If you're feeling a bit wobbly...

By Holly Bramwell

If you're feeling a bit wobbly...

Copyright © 2020 Holly Bramwell

Published by Starkidworks

Buckshaw Village, UK

For Ellie, Sophie & Finley

If you're feeling a bit wobbly...

Just wanted to check in with you,
make sure you're doing ok.
If you're feeling a bit wobbly,
remember you're loved, every day.

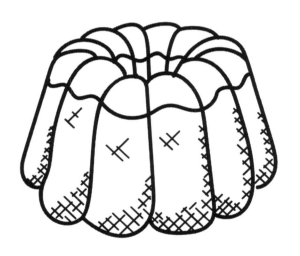

It's ok if you don't want to talk today,

just know there are people

out there who will listen to you,

when you are ready.

Nobody expects you to be perfect,
so stop putting pressure on yourself.

If you have managed to do just one
good thing for yourself today,
then that is a huge achievement.

Night In

Kettle on, cup of tea,
comfy throws and watch TV.

The dog curled up around my feet,
there is no place I'd rather be.

Be that person who you always needed
when you were a child.

Just one positive comment,
a hug and a smile,
can make a huge difference in a child's life.

When all this is over,
I will hug you
for a little bit longer.

Help you Grow

When you're finding it hard to face the world,
Stop. Take a moment. Breathe.

There is always someone out there
who will care for you,
will get you through this,
help you grow,
plant new seeds.

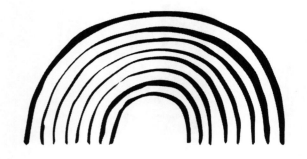

Sunshine and Rainbows

Life isn't all sunshine and rainbows,
some days can be really tough; hard going,
but when you have good people in your world,
It warms the heart,
reminds you they're worth knowing.

When life gives you lemons,
add them to your gin!

Not everything needs to be
dealt with today!

Dear Parents and Carers:

Don't ever feel guilty about
having a little time out to
recharge your batteries.

In order to do this job,
you need your
health and happiness.

When the Streets are Home

As you settle down for the evening,
heating on, warm drink in hand,
please take a moment to think of those,
whose beds are cold; it wasn't planned.

You see everyone has a story,
and it's so easy to turn a blind eye,
so when you walk past the stranger on the street,
take a moment. Think.
Don't let it pass you by.

Say hello, shake their hand,
offer a blanket, a drink, some food,
they are a person, with a heart and soul,
just these small gestures will lift their mood.

If more people start to think this way,
imagine the difference it could make.
It only takes a moment of your time,
after all, life is a bit of give and take.

Remembrance

A moment to remember those who fought for us all,
they are in our hearts, souls we never met,
a minute of silence is only small,
but we stand silent, Lest We Forget.

Show one act of kindness every day.
It doesn't matter how small.
You can make a huge difference.

People come and go,
but the person you see in the mirror,
will be with you forever.

Take care of them.

The Dream

Have you ever had an idea, a dream,
but it seemed too hard to begin?
Or you thought, someone else will do it,
I don't have the time, or the courage within.

Well if everyone thought this way,
we wouldn't experience new things.
Just the same thing day in, day out,
so challenge yourself, see what it brings.

Bright Star

When you look up at the clear night sky,
and there's a blanket of stars in view,
remember they are all bright and unique,
they shine so much, just like you.

If you are ever in any doubt of who to trust,
TRUST YOU.
You know YOU better than anyone!

Giving up a little bit of time
to help someone else out,
is the most generous thing you can do.

Take a Chance

Take a chance on something in your life,
for we only live once on this Earth.
Be creative, learn and share knowledge,
you are important, know your worth.

Unique

Embrace your uniqueness every day,
the differences make you who you are!

Who wants to follow the crowd anyway?
Give life everything you've got, you're a star!

Be kind.

Check in with family and friends.

Don't leave it too late.

Money is short-lived.

New houses are short-lived.

New cars are short-lived.

Kindness is everlasting.

Day Off

Take a 'day off' from the world now and then,
have some quiet time on your own, take care.
Don't worry, no one will judge you for it,
it can be weird and 'peopley' out there!

Young Carers

You're an inspiration to us every day,
with your amazing acts of kindness.
You always put their needs first,
show others what it means to be selfless.

We're sorry you miss out on things,
and have had to grow up so fast.
We wish we could give you that time back,
but know some things remain in the past.

You show others what it means to be a carer,
teaching them about disabilities every day.
Opening their eyes to the daily struggles,
you say what others are too scared to say.

As you continue to grow up in this complex world,
you'll face challenges that are hard to climb.
But, remember you have an amazing power,
to love, to care, to give others your time.

The World is a better place with you in it.

You are loved.

Share your light and help others,
but be sure to let it reflect,
to help you shine.

Yorkshire Tea

When I wake up in the morning,
I need a decent brew,
I converted a few years ago,
from the rival county, who knew!

Yes, I'm a Lancashire lass,
but can't resist this tea I have,
love to those on t'other side,
you've created magic in a bag!

Tired

If you're feeling tired and weary,
slow down and take a break.

It's important to look after yourself,
some other things can wait.

Hang in there,

you are doing an amazing job!

Use this time to read,

try cooking something new,

paint that room you kept meaning to tackle,

have a clothes sort out,

switch off the TV and play board games,

learn and new skill online,

have more hugs with your family,

eat and drink plenty,

rest.

Happy is...

Listening to your favourite song,
Spending time with your kids/pets,
Going for a walk,
Reading a great book,
Watching a fab film,
Eating your favourite food,
Talking to a friend,
Hugs.

Wheelchair Woes

You must have been distracted,
and that's why you didn't see,
that you'd mounted half the pavement,
now where does that leave me?

Yep, now I'm cruising down the road,
fearing for my life,
so please park a little better,
and save all this trouble and strife!

Change of Weather

It may be cold and windy,
and the skies are moody and grey,
but you are the storyteller for your life,
so paint rainbows and sunshine today.

Things I would say to my younger self...

1. You can accomplish anything,
   just give it some thought.

2. You are worth more than you think,
   don't put yourself down.

3. You will always have someone in your life
   who loves you.

4. You should never underestimate
   the need for sleep!

Showing you care helps mend the heart a little.

Child in Lockdown

I know life is hard at the moment little one,
you miss your family, teacher and friends,
their hugs, love, fun and laughter,
not really knowing when this will end.

So I want you to know you can talk to me,
let me know you're feeling sad,
I will always listen and I will try to help,
for this is cherished time we've never had.

And when the day comes, of what'll be a new normal,
I will still be here to help you find your way.
The world will feel like a different place,
but we'll just take our time, day by day.

Colour Forecast

Some days can feel grizzly and grey,
some can feel blurry and blue.
So I am your sunshine and yellow,
to make you happy and smile too!

Christmas Time

Christmas markets, school fairs,
mulled wine, party hair.
Letters to Santa, put the tree up,
novelty jumpers, warm drinks to sup.

Although this is a busy time of year,
please remember those you love so dear.
Catch up with friends you haven't seen in a while,
and enjoy the festive season with a smile!

Respect

Teach our children about the world,
about the importance of RESPECT...
That your friends can be black, brown or white,
a woman can love a woman, a man love a man,
this is perfectly alright.
That some people can't walk, talk or hear your voice,
but they ARE people with feelings,
they need to be heard,
society can help, let's make the right choice.

That it's ok to share your thoughts
and speak your mind,
remind them they are the future of this world,
Let's teach them good values,
to always be kind.

Lancashire Lass

I'm a Lancashire Lass, born 'n' bred,
where the Pendle witches lived (enough said)!
Where dinner is tea, tea is a brew,
well... that's just my point of view!

Ask the kids, do you live in a barn?
In and out of rooms... (just keep calm)!
When it gets dark (probably around 1),
then that's the time to stick the big light on!

Ok, so it's mainly grey and drizzly up north,
topics of conversation are weather
and grub, of course!
But we're the nicest people I have to say,
so together, let's celebrate 'Lancashire Day!'

Once upon a time
there was a woman who
liked writing and drinking tea.
It was me.

The End